A BOY WITH FLAWS

THE STORY OF EVERY CHILD

ANISH SWARNKAR

ISBN 979-888521944-0

I like to dedicate this book to my friends , family and

teachers who motivated me to write this wonderful book
in

my life . And to each and every one who

is reading this book .

Contents

Preface

One day in November 2021 I and my old
friends were just talking about our school
days, what we did in our old school, most
of the timepass our favorite thing, and the
things we love to do the most. many of the
mischief we used to do, who we used to
taunt the most, and how our lives changed.
After a long conversation with my friends about
our childhood, I got the idea of
writing a book from the starting of my school life
till it changed because of flaws I did.
The title A Boy With Flaws came from the
story of my life. This is because at every
point in life I have done many mistakes and
always have been taunted for my mistakes.
In this book, I have shared some part and tails
of my life which is full of flaws and even
some of these teach many moral values of life.
I hope you enjoy to read this book based on
life of a boy full of flaws.

Prologue

A Boy With Flaws

-Anish Swarnkar

Once, there was a boy who lived in a small town in
Jharkhand dreamed big and even bigger than his size.
When he was just 1-1.5 years old he loved to have
screwdrivers and
play with them. Time! greatest thing in world passed
very
smoothly and he grew in a very healthy environment.
At very first stage he was good at studies. The family
members of that boy thought that he is so focused in
his studies so , they asked that little fellow what's his
aim in life
in which profession he wants to be . But
this was not so simple and he said just changed
everyone's thinking about him.
Without thinking too much he said with a pure soul
"dad I just want to be in my own I want create my own
creations, I want to make my own cars which no
one have even dreamed" and at this point everyone
was
speechless.
And his story begins....

Introduction

Every person to whom this question arise that who is this
boy, for those- it was me

1
Change In School

When I was just 5-6 years old my performance
'was dropping rapidly and I was performing
worse and worse in my annual exams.
My dad was too strict about my studies. He took
a decision that changed my life. Previously I was
in a local school with very little facility, so my
dad changed my school to one of the best schools
of that time. When my school was changed I was
too scared, the only thing in my mind was the
poor marks which I got in my exams in my previous
school. But then also I was trying my best as a student
of UKG (under kindergarten). And then my UKG
was successfully completed and even with good
grades. My dad was so happy that he took me to
the toy shop and bought me the best and most
costly car available. When I was too happy he just
said: "Son don't be so happy there's a lot of things
to achieve it's just a starting ". And these words
just changed my thinking about my dad.
And then my real school life started.

Student Life

The light,

The glory.

The fairytale story.

The mystery I say,

We did those days.

Jumping on mud,

following the cars.

Sitting on school bus,

which takes too far.

Jumping on seats,

happiness, and greets.

Sharing our treats,

whenever we meet.

Lunch was disaster,

running so faster.

Playing hide and seek,

like some freaks.

Last period was fair,

roaming here and there.

the principal on round,

everyone underground.

And here comes the closing time,

the best moment in student life.

Smile on face,

in every case.

Bag mouth open,

empty stomach ache.

Going home,

without any tension.

Commenting on rotating wheels,

was our part-time occupation.

Yeah, you are right,

these are the small kids,

where everything is right.

again,

Jumping on mud,

following the cars.

Sitting on school bus,

which takes too far.

But here the situation was different.

happiness becomes sadness and anger,

greetings has came to an end and fly.

Lunch was faster,

competition was vaster.

hide and seek becomes

hide from everyone and seek each one.

Last period is still a fair,

Roaming here and there.

Principal on round,

no one underground.

here comes closing time,

everyone comes out.

Nothing is left,

no happiness, no shout.

Now nothing is right,

everything ends with a fight.

Bunking school and tuition has become an art,

showing others how you are smart.

Yeah you are right ,

these are the grown one ,

doing flaws in there lives.

-Anish Swarnkar

2
Beginning of School Life

Time changes everything and it changed again.
As I entered class 1 I made friends but not the
real ones.they behaved like I am having no importance
in their life.But after some months I was so happy
I made true friends, friendsfor those cast, colour
and money doesn't matter.Again time passed so
gracefully and we grew nicelybut now the environment
was not so healthy.In our group, only 4 members
were left Prem, Harsh, Pratik and Me.Our bond became
so strong that if one of us were in a problem
our whole group was worried and we all solved it
together.
No one can touch us on the school campus. We became
the most unwanted students at that time.
My thinking about exams changed I was only interested
in
just the exam my grade was becoming poorer every year.
My family was too upset about my result.
To solve this problem and to make me mature I
was given a chance.I got an opportunity to play cricket.
And then Cricket entered my life.

3
Entry Of Cricket

When I was in class 3 I was too much interested in cricket. As I said to my father he said in a very strict way "you have to manage your studies as well as cricket at the same time ". I was so happy the next day my dad took me to a cricket academy named BCCC. The coach's name was Suresh sir. He was so polite to me that I can't even explain. Because of him, I became a noob to pro. He helped in every instant in my life, he always supported me. He just wanted me to perform well. The entry of cricket was like a changing point for me, It just changed me for a while. In India, in every town in every next house, there is one who wants to be a cricketer And after having this much competition My chance of becoming a cricketer Was next to impossible. But then also after practicing for 3 years, It was my last year playing cricket in the category of under 14. That year was too special for me because the captain of my team was no other than me and myself. And when I was going to play my first match as a caption an incident occurred.

4
The Incident

It's a fact,

When everything is going alright
and there are no problems in life.
We must understand that something
disastrous is going to happen.

One day before Holika, me and my local friends
made a plan to play cricket on the ground near my home
named mines rescue ground.
When I asked my mom that may I go to play
The next morning, She strictly refused me.
She said "you don't have to go the environment there is
not good there and you have to study also because you
will not be able to study if the tournament will start "
And then the making of mistakes started
and I made one of the biggest mistake in my life
I slept last night late because I was too relaxed
and confirmed that I am not going to play the
next morning. The next morning, the time was
approx 4:15 when one of my friends Yash called me
on my cellphone and said "bro come fast we are
waiting for you, come fast or the match will start ."

I said, "sorry bro I can't come today I mom has said
not to go today I have to study." He pleased me and said,
"it's an important match today with a local team and
if you play your practice for the tournament will
also be done ." And at this moment I made the biggest
mistake ever, I said them ok and went to the ground
without informing my mom. disobeying my mom
was the worst choice of my mom.It paid me soon.
Due to sleeping late I was too sleepy,
I was not even concentrated in in-game.
and when I was batting that happened which no
one has even thought, while batting a bouncer
ball was delivered by the baller. I was too sleepy
that the ball just hit me before I could even judge,
and hit me like a bullet. It injured me internally.
At the time I felt nothing at all but then also my
friends suggested me to take a rest.
Everything was fine, I slept peacefully. When I
wake up the next day, I found myself in hospital.
Everything just changed in one day.
The doctor said that I has been injured internally,
and even the worst was it affected my brain.
The doctor strictly prohibited me from doing too
much physical work, like playing cricket, football,
etc. That night just changed my life.
And because of it, I have to leave cricket for a few
years.I was too sad, this heartbreaking moment
was too much painful.
"The sky wept,
Earth's heart also melted.
The silence screamed everything,
life became like has been in contact with the Bunya tree.
Each and every drop of water from the eye

can explain the pain ."

5
Greatest Healer

Time the greatest healer can heal anything,
It can even heal that wounds can't be healed
by medicine. Time changes everything and it
changed again but now in a good way. Time
passed I was again on track. Everyone in my
family as well as my friends helped me a lot to
recover myself. Now my interest changed,
I was interested in martial arts. I was not so
strong yet, but then also I joined Dhanbad Public
School's martial art classes. And my teacher was
Pandey sir. He was also very helpful,
he always supported me in my practice and always
motivated me.
My next <u>mistake</u> -
I forget to take permission from my father.
Again everything was going alright.
s we know, **when everything is right,**
something disastrous is going to happen.
And hence disaster happened.
A national-level boxing competition was organized.
I was also selected for it but in the category of beginners.

We had started our practice one month before.
We were practicing too hard
and were fully prepared for the tournament.
only 3-4 days were left for the tournament when I finally
told my father about my martial arts practice,
I was too -too scared that what will he say.
And that only thing that I was thinking not to happen,
just happened.
He said you are not fully recovered yet,
You are not participating in the tournament.
I accepted his words because he said this after thinking
of my health.
For some moment I felt bad, but after some days I was
back in my daily routine.
I started enjoying my life.
After few months I was 13 .
My perfrmance in class 6 at that time was ok not too bad
not too good .
At this time I was at adolescent age ,
So distraction was common .
And here the next chapter begin.

Love

LOVE is life ,

LOVE is light,

Love can change the mood to fight.

When at first look ,

You forget about the background ,

Everything is silent ,

There's left no sound.

Everything becomes blur,

No matter what's on ground.

The onl questin in mind ,

Will she be mine.

-ANISH SWARNKAR

6

Distraction

In my life, these were the most beautiful days.
There was a smile at every point of time.
The anger inside me was gone, everyone was shocked
to see my behavior. I was not the old aggressive Anish
I was changed. And the reason behind It was a girl
named 'Shreya'. And you know the funniest thing,
I was the person she hated the most. When we were
in class 3or4, she was the monitor of the class and I
was a person who wrote very slowly and most of
my work remained incomplete, SO, the teacher used
to give her duty to help me to complete my work.
And that was one of the reasons why she hated me
because to help me in completing my work it cost a
games period. And according to me, I enjoyed
spending time with her. My next mistake was I

never ask her for friendship. I always thought that
as I accept her as my friend, one day she will also
accept me. but this day never came, we reached
class 5. This was the final year we were together but her
hate rate for me increased day by day.
Days passed and the final exams came, and that
moment also came that I never wanted to come.
On the day of the last exam, it was my birthday,
So, I had to go to distribute toffies to all teachers.
There was a rule in my school that one can take a
student with him or her to distribute toffies.
When the teacher asked whom I want to take
with me, Without thinking too much
I said "ma'am Shreya " I don't know why but she
simply said "eew no".
That moment was one of the worst moment
s in my life. That year it was the first time I cried
on my birthday. After the bell rang one of my
friends told me that she said me that because of my
sink tone. At that moment I felt soo bad that I can't
even explain. So, exams passed our result was out
and all were promoted to the next class and got
separated in girls block and boys block.
I was in boy's block and she was in girl's block.
BUT then also to impress her I had always been
participating in competitions, and the best thing
was I was always 1 rank above her in every
competition and this thing always frustrated her.
I didn't even get to know that when this fight for
her became an attraction for me. Day by day I was
getting attracted to her more strongly. This
attraction was too strong that I have said to my friends
that she is my girlfriend and I love her. But on

another side the situation was fully different
there she didn't even want to see my face.
But we say "love is blind ". So this one-sided
love inside me was increasing day by day and
the only person who knew this was Susan.
What can I say to him a friend or an enemy
when we were in class 8 he was in a singing
group and Shreya was also one of the members
of that singing group. So he did the work of petrol
in the fire, he proposed Shreya and the worst
the thing was she also accepted his proposal
for the first few months, I didn't even talk to Susan
but then suddenly one day he said " I have talked
to Sherya about your friendship and she has said
ok I will talk to him" after listening to these words
from the happiness, I was like a helium balloon flying
high in the sky. The next day he said "she will talk
to you in night camp" so participate in night camp.
I said ok as her wish. So we participated in the night
camp as soon as I reached school I saw
Susan in front of the gate. he said let all the girls come
from the girl's block then we will talk. I again said ok.
After a few hours, I saw her
'coming down from stairs as fairies come from heaven,
her hair was waving in the air reminding dark
beautiful night, her face was like fairies in fairy tails,
her lips were red like rose, In one word she was
looking like the most beautiful creature I ever seen on
earth whom God had made himself.
She came slowly towards me and this was the
first time she talked to me politely. She said "
on your birthday I didn't say eew because of you
actually that time I was talking to my friend and

I said eww to her not you but after some time I
listened to what you have said to everyone that I am
your girlfriend I was too much angry and I wanted
to abuse you a lot ". I simply said sorry and started
talking to her and from this time I changed. All my
tension was gone I was too happy and distraction
was at its peak. from this time I was behaving Like
PK in love is waste of time, To see her I and my
friends had our lunch near the girl's block gate.
At the end of our ground, I started doing extra classes
to meet her on the school bus. One day in the morning
when she entered the bus everyone was wishing her a
happy birthday and the day was 25 July 2018. when I got
to know that her birthday was on that day. That day I
was
feeling very ashamed that I don't know her birthday,
from
that day I didn't even talk to her and she also started
ignoring me but we say no one-sided lover is mad, I
started
finding her on Facebook from my friend's account. After
some days of finding her, I finally found her, after 3 days
I found her account it was again her birthday. when I
said
her that I am Anish she directly blocked me but the
madness inside me was soo big that I requested all my
friends and classmates who know her and talk to her to
wish her birthday from my side and guess what
happened
next. She blocked half of them and the rest was
threatened
to never say anything about me to her. since then I
always

used to see her like thieves I always used to ask about her
from Susan and he always asked me that why do you
care
about her when she doesn't even want to see you and I
always used to say him a thing bro it is true love what
happened when she doesn't like me but whatever
happens, I will always love her no matter what. Even
I have not talked to her for more than 5 years but then
also there is not a single day in which I have thinked
about her.

7
Biggest Flaw

<u>The biggest mistake that a student do in this stage is being involved in everything except studies.</u> After being involved in all these things the only thing I was taking too light was my studies and the result of ignoring and not giving importance to my studies was here. I failed my final exam of class 9 and I was given two options the first option was to repeat my class 9 and the second option was to change my school and repeat class 9. I was t being able to do eye contact with my friends and the neighbors. So to avoid my friends I chose the second option and to avoid neighbors I started to be in my home I rarely used to go outside so that no one asks me anything about my result. I was fully depressed I didn't even know what to do next. But as we say there is a will there is a way. I studied day and night at one of the top schools in Dhanbad but now I was in a school which don't even have a proper playground. Sometimes it's not like that as we see it when it was my first day in school I made everyone in the class my friend. The environment was too friendly and the

teachers were also too co-operative. Bt the only problem in this school was that it was co-ed and I was never comfortable with girls. The teachers helped me a lot to pass my annual exams in class nine. Because of their help the person who was not being able to score more than 40% got more than 85%. This year I met teachers who changed my thinking about teachers try made me realize that teachers can be friends within a limit. This year also taught me how we can shut up the mouth of others who taunt us about our bad results.
Again,

> *When everything is going alright*
> *and there are no problems in life.*
> *We must understand that something*
> *disastrous is going to happen.*
> This time not only for me but this time disaster for the whole planet occurred. That is covid-19.............

Failed but not Faliour

Do well try hard never leave hard work apart,

If you succeed you will get the fame, name, and aim.

So, focus on your aim leave all shame on what others think and say.

These are the things that all say.

<u>*But no one teaches us what to do if we do not succeed or we fail.*</u>

From teachers to relatives very far,

everyone is too rude and hars.

The taunts, lectures, and late-night thoughts,

make us knock doors to the dark.

The pain we get the depression we feel,

no one cares because we failed .

We failed exams, we failed race of life, we failed to fight against life,

we failed.

But what about the hard work we did,

what about the fight we fought against the time just to reach our goal.

Was all those wasted was all those not so good to succeed,

Am I a failure...

At this moment everything disguise headache rises brain becomes tight,

the only thing left is to do suicide.

But what will happen even after suicide,

first they taunted you then they will taunt your dear pop's.

The game is still the same till now you have not lost the game,

just lag behind it's your time to shine.

Shut their mouth,

show them out.

That I have just failed but I am not a failure.

-Anish Swarnkar

Moral

*Whatever happens, it's for you. If something
bad happens you must understand that you are
going to learn the great moral value of life which
no one can teach except the flaws that you
make in your life. Keep making mistakes do flaws in
life because these will teach you the real values of life,
they will teach you how to correct your mistake and how
to handle even worst situations.*

Readers

If you liked reading this book please give your precious feedback in my email (swarnkaranish@gmail.com).

If you want the next part then, please send part-2 in the same email.

Thanking You

Anish Swarnkar